Sex, Shopping
& Chocolate

Sex, Shopping & Chocolate

The Hilarious World of Dot

Daphne David

INDEX

First published 1996 by Boxtree Limited in association with Paperlink Limited,
356 Kennington Road, London SE11 4LD

This edition published 2002 for Index Books Limited by Boxtree
an imprint of Pan Macmillan Ltd
Pan Macmillan, 20 New Wharf Road, London N1 9RR
Basingstoke and Oxford
Associated companies throughout the world
www.panmacmillan.com

ISBN 0 7522 1125 0

9 8 7 6 5 4 3 2 1

A CIP catalogue record for this book is available from the British Library.

Printed by Mackays of Chatham

Dot's worst fears
about the supermodel party
were confirmed.

'Ok!' Said Dot purposefully. 'I've sniffed the flowers and eaten the chocolates. Now I want to see some commitment!'

Dot arrived late at Roger's
dinner party: She was determined
to punish him for scoffing at her
when she said she had
nothing to wear.

'Dot!' Cried the voice
of the cream cake.
'Dot, it's me you love!'

'All right' agreed Dot reluctantly,
'it was better than a poke in the
eye with a sharp stick. But only
because it was quicker'.

'Well, that's the housework done,'
said Dot cheerfully.

Dot was on the horns of a
dilemma: Was she to talk or
was she to suck her cheeks
in for the rest of the night?

'Flowers shmowers! Snapped Dot.
'If you really loved me
you'd clean out the bath
and cook supper.'

Gavin's behaviour became
increasingly odd after he discovered
Dot was earning more than him.

'A bloody woman driver?
Correct!'. Said Dot drily.
'But do you know what this is?'

Although Dot
was against 'animal testing',
she couldn't resist trying
a little Night Repair Cream on Fifi.

Dot reacted badly
when Dick announced
their relationship was over.

Dot's step aerobics class was
just round the corner,
yet it still took her
4 years to get there.

'I shop and I shop! Wailed Dot!
'And I still have nothing to wear!'

Dot was not going to jeopardize
the success of her dinner party
by serving food.

Dot was curious to know
if the workmen would still
whistle at her after she sawed
the legs off their scaffolding.

Dot made the mistake
of giving her mother
the office fax number.

'They're for a friend!' Shrieked Dot,
as she dropped the
flavoured condoms into her bag.

'Don't be ridiculous!' Snapped Dot.
'How can I come in when there's
a woman in there wearing
an identical dress to mine?!'

'But I fancy him!' Shrieked Dot,
as she dragged the handsome
stranger off the bus.

Over and over Dot repeated:
"A child is for life not just
for Christmas"...

Dot had always dreaded the day
a job interview would coincide
with a touch of Pre-Menstrual Tension.

'I'm sorry,' said Dot, 'but this is
what I do to skinny people
who say they have
a weight problem.'

The men talked about fishing
and the women talked
about the men.

'My God', thought Dot, 'they
really do talk bollocks on the
washing up liquid commercials.'

It was one of life's
happy coincidences – Dot was
carrying some oven cleaner
when the flasher appeared.

Dot could not control herself—
it was just one 'Yo ho ho'
too many.

There were some days
when Dot's hormones seemed
to have a life of their own.

Dot spoke slowly so everybody could understand: "This is a floor", she said, "these are clothes, and Lo! Over yonder is a dirty wash basket".

'For pity's sake, groaned Dot,
'a bunch of flowers and
a box of chocolates
would've been fine.'

It may be the season of goodwill
thought Dot but it's also
the season of going crazy
and buying crap.

Dot's one and only attempt
at finding her 'G' spot
led to an embarrassing
night in casualty.

'I know it's not a fancy dress party!'
Snapped Dot.
'I'm not in fancy dress.'

'Don't be silly! Giggled Dot.
'Of course I wouldn't bring
the kitchen sink on holiday.
I've brought the nice pink one
from the bathroom.'

What a perfect world this is
thought Dot. The sun is shining
and I'm a bitch in a big car.

Dot showed Helen the new man
in her life. 'Go on,' she prompted,
'ask me how I got him in there.'

When Dot first discovered Eric
in her favourite summer dress
she was deeply upset.
'How could you wear it
without a belt?' She sobbed.

In the nick of time, Dot remembered
she had some Evening Primrose oil
in her handbag.

Dot finally found a way
to stop the puppy
stealing the loo paper.

Finally Dot spoke: Do I get my
birthday kiss or are we just going
to lean on this fence all day?'

n aerobics video! For me?' Gasped Dot.
'Oh Barry, you shouldn't have.'

'Oh really!' Snarled Dot, 'I can get
chocolates and flowers anytime
—how about some cash
and rampant sex.'

Dot enjoyed spring cleaning.
It gave her a rare opportunity
to beat the living crap
out of something.

'We're quite informal here', said Dot,
'you may call me "madam"
or "your highness".'

Though the bathroom mirror
could never lie, Dot consoled herself
with the thought that it could
be smashed to pieces
with a chair leg.

Dot thought it was a pity
that she couldn't make love
in the surf without getting
sand in her gusset.

Dot always offered
the children a choice:
Fishfingers or unimaginable violence.

Just minutes into the presentation,
Dot realized both her shoulder pads
were on one shoulder.

Dot was thrilled
with the results of her diet.

'Tell me', asked Dot, 'are you
paid extra to be unpleasant
or does it come naturally?'

Lost in Brett's powerful embrace,
Dot struggled heroically to reach
the bit of spinach
stuck in her teeth.

As the moody silences grew longer,
Dot realized this was not
the Gavin she married.

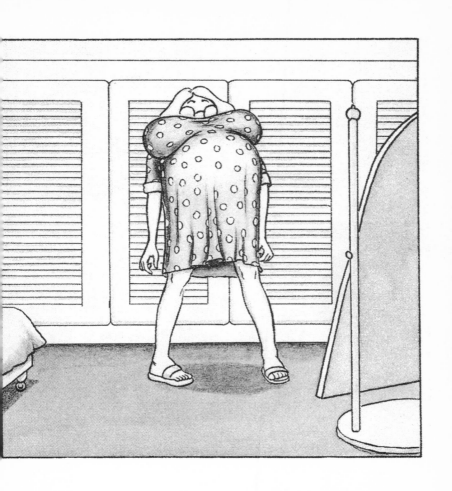

'Will I ever regain my figure?'
Thought Dot. 'Or am I
to become one of
life's forgotten profiterôles?'

It was Dot's turn to indulge in
her Valentine's day fantasy:
A tub of ice-cream and a video.

The label on Gavin's underpants
said "handwash only."
'who are they trying to kid?'
growled Dot.

'It's a strange world', mused Dot,
'where one woman's breast implant
is another woman's executive toy'.

'My politics are changing!'Shouted
Dot. 'I think a woman's place *is*
in the home – but a man's
is in the garden shed!'

As time passed
Dot became quite adept
at juggling work and home life.

Sometimes Dot wanted
to hear 'delicious' instead of 'good'.

Dot knew that some men needed gentle persuasion before they showed their true feelings.

At least Dot
got her foot in the door
of the Botticelli Modelling Agency.

To her horror Dot realized
Brian really did want to
to show her his etchings.

For years Dot had wanted to
'frizz' up her bank manager's hair.

There was something wrong
and Dot felt sure
Howard was suppressing it.

Using some industrial strength polythene, Dot rustled up some inexpensive crêche facilities.

There was something about
her non-sexist, vegetarian date
that made Dot want to strip
and eat a raw steak.

Dot jumped onto the catwalk.
'For pity's sake!' She cried.
'Somebody buy this poor girl
a decent meal!'

Dot did not subscribe to
the theory that timing was
the art of comedy,
and pressed on with
her treefrog impression.

Dot's parents gave Gavin
a somewhat cautious welcome.

It was Dot's job to prepare
the stationery cupboard for
the office party.

Dot had to impress upon Gavin
that he couldn't just call
whenever he felt like it.

Instead of a menu Dot gave
the family a list of topics
not to be discussed during
Christmas lunch.

'You don't have to give me your seat because I'm a woman,' whispered Dot. 'You have to give it to me because I'm a working mother and I may go crazy if you don't.'

Dot decided to stick up for men:
'Of course men would be good at
having babies — they have
smaller brains so would
feel less pain.'

Dot was fed up with the childish
innuendo: 'Go on!' She snapped.
'Get your dick out and we'll
have an even bigger laugh!'

Dot wished she could
remember a few clever
put-down lines.

Dot made a fool of herself
in the art gallery
by admiring the fire alarm.

On Christmas morning
Dot came downstairs
like a little child.

Just days before the holiday,
Dot tried to develop a likeness
to her passport photograph.

Dot went into some detail
on her preparation of the
pudding only to discover
she'd forgotten to unwrap it.

Dot had to be honest with herself:
Was it worth dating Zorg
just to make Brian jealous?

Just because Dot was on holiday
didn't mean she had to let
herself go.

He seemed every girl's dream,
But Dot had to be sure
in her own mind.

Dot bitterly regretted buying panty shields with little wings.

Dot's spirits were lifted
when, one day, her husband
came home from work.

It was a relief to Dot
that Fifi enjoyed
bungee rope jumping.

All attempts by
the gynaecologist's assistant
to relax Dot failed.

Some days
Dot couldn't be bothered
to put a face on.

During the flight to Málaga,
Dot convinced herself
she had left the iron on.

'Should I lie?' Thought Dot.
'Or should I tell Brian
that I have been
deliberately avoiding him?'